The Scientists Behind
The
Environment

Robert Snedden

LB OF BARKING & DAGENHAM LIBRARIES	
9060000046208	
Bertrams	04/04/2012
JN	£8.99
J333.72	

BA

D1322843

906 000 000 46208

www.raintreepublishers.co.uk
Visit our website to find out
more information about
Raintree books.

To order:
☎ Phone 0845 6044371
🖷 Fax +44 (0) 1865 312263
🖳 Email myorders@raintreepublishers.co.uk

Customers from outside the UK please telephone +44 1865 312262

Raintree is an imprint of Capstone Global Library Limited,
a company incorporated in England and Wales having its
registered office at 7 Pilgrim Street, London, EC4V 6LB –
Registered company number: 6695582

Text © Capstone Global Library Limited 2011
First published in hardback in 2011
Paperback edition first published in 2012
The moral rights of the proprietor have been asserted.

All rights reserved. No part of this publication may be
reproduced in any form or by any means (including
photocopying or storing it in any medium by electronic
means and whether or not transiently or incidentally to
some other use of this publication) without the written
permission of the copyright owner, except in accordance
with the provisions of the Copyright, Designs and
Patents Act 1988 or under the terms of a licence
issued by the Copyright Licensing Agency, Saffron
House, 6–10 Kirby Street, London EC1N 8TS (www.cla.
co.uk). Applications for the copyright owner's written
permission should be addressed to the publisher.

Edited by Andrew Farrow, Adam Miller, and
 Diyan Leake
Designed by Philippa Jenkins
Original illustrations © Capstone Global Library
 Limited 2011
Illustrated by Stefan Chubluk and Capstone Global
 Library Limited
Picture research by Hannah Taylor
Originated by Capstone Global Library Limited
Printed and bound in China by CTPS

ISBN 978 1 406 22059 9 (hardback)
14 13 12 11 10
10 9 8 7 6 5 4 3 2 1

ISBN 978 1 406 22187 9 (paperback)
15 14 13 12 11
10 9 8 7 6 5 4 3 2 1

British Library Cataloguing in Publication Data
 Snedden, Robert.
  The scientists behind the environment. -- (Sci-hi)
  333.7'2'0922-dc22
A full catalogue record for this book is available from the
British Library.

Acknowledgements
The author and publishers are grateful to the following
for permission to reproduce copyright material: Alamy
Images pp. **8** (© Robert Harding Picture Library Ltd), **22**
(© Tim Cuff); Bridgeman Art Library p. **24** (© Trustees of
the Watts Gallery, Compton, Surrey, UK); Corbis pp. **4–5**
(Christopher Talbot Frank), **9** (Bettmann), **16** (epa/Jessica
Gow), **38** (Micheline Pelletier); FLPA p. **5** inset (Mark
Moffett/Minden Pictures); Getty Images pp. **15** (Time
Life Pictures/Alfred Eisenstaedt), **28** (WireImage/Jordin
Althaus), **32** (AFP/Lionel Bonaventure); istockphoto
p. **11** (© Ron and Patty Thomas Photography); Library
of Congress p. **10**; NASA **contents page** top, pp. **20**,
21, **23**, **27** (Goddard Space Flight Center Scientific
Visualization Studio), **30**, **31**; Nicolas Faivre p. **7**); Reuters
p. **34** (Gustau Nacarino); Rex Features p. **35** (Sipa Press);
Science Photo Library pp. **12–13** (Farrell Grehan), **14** (US
Fish and Wildlife Service), **33** (Reporters/Claire Deprez),
37 (George Bernard), **41** (Martin Shields); shutterstock
background images and design elements throughout,
contents page bottom (© Pakhnyushcha), pp. **6**
(© 26ISO), **36** (© Chris Taylor), **17** (© Pakhnyushcha), **19**
(©zcw/© Ljupco Smokovski/© FormosanFish/© Milos
Luzanin).

Main cover photograph of a scientist studying plant
diversity after a fire in Emas National Park, Brazil
reproduced with permission of FLPA (Frans Lanting);
inset cover photograph of a bee on a crocus reproduced
with permission of istockphoto (© Willi Scmitz).

The publisher would like to thank literary consultant
Marla Conn and content consultant Michael Bright for
their assistance in the preparation of this book.

Every effort has been made to contact copyright holders
of material reproduced in this book. Any omissions will
be rectified in subsequent printings if notice is given to
the publisher.

Disclaimer
All the Internet addresses (URLs) given in this book were
valid at the time of going to press. However, due to the
dynamic nature of the Internet, some addresses may
have changed, or sites may have changed or ceased to
exist since publication. While the author and publisher
regret any inconvenience this may cause readers, no
responsibility for any such changes can be accepted by
either the author or the publisher.

Contents

Who took this picture? Find out on page 20!

How do honeybees help environmental scientists? Turn to page 17 to find out!

Some words are shown in bold, **like this**. These words are explained in the glossary. You will find important information and definitions underlined, <u>like this</u>.

What is THE ENVIRONMENT?

We read and hear a lot about the environment in the news. Often we're told that we should do what we can to protect it. But what do we actually mean by "the environment"?

Your environment is everything around you. It includes all the other living things you come into contact with, such as birds, bugs, and your buddies! It also includes all the non-living things, such as the air you breathe, the water you drink, and the materials that make your home. The exhaust fumes from cars are as much a part of the environment as the trees in the park. The weather is part of your environment, too.

Sometimes scientists have to get into tricky places to do their research. This one is dangling from a tree in the rainforests of Colombia, South America.

Every living thing is part of its environment. The environment of a fish might be the ocean or a river. An eagle's environment might be the rocks and skies of a mountain range. The environment can be as small as the rock under which a tiny insect lives, or as big as the whole world.

This book will look at just a few of the many people who have worked to help us understand the environment. It is a big and complex subject, and many scientists, with many different skills, work together to study it.

DIFFERENT ENVIRONMENTS

Scientists studying the environment will often divide it into different parts.

- **The NATURAL ENVIRONMENT includes the huge variety of relationships between living things and their surroundings.**

- **The PHYSICAL ENVIRONMENT is the non-living part of the environment. It includes water, air, rocks and soils, light and temperature.**

- **The BUILT ENVIRONMENT is the one we humans have made for ourselves. It includes roads, buildings and other structures that make up our towns and cities.**

LEARNING ABOUT THE ENVIRONMENT

We can look at the environment in very many ways. An environmental scientist might study geography, chemistry, physics, **geology**, and engineering, as well as biology.

ENVIRONMENTAL GEOGRAPHY

Environmental geographers look at the relationships between humans and their surroundings and the ways in which human activities can change the landscape. Dr Tim Stojanovic of the University of St Andrews is an environmental geographer with a special interest in the impact of humans on coasts. He recognizes the huge international team effort that is involved in environmental research: "My work often involves large teams looking at the unique challenges facing the marine and coastal environment."

ECOLOGY

The study of the relationships between living things and their environment is called **ecology**. Living things are said to be adapted to their environment. An **adaptation** is something that helps a living thing to survive where it lives. The gills of a fish adapt it for life in water, for example.

FIRE ECOLOGY

Fire ecologists study the effects fire has on plants and animals and their environment. A big fire sweeping through a forest or grassland can be one of the worst things that could happen, but it may have some benefits, too. A fire can clear old, dead wood. The ash left behind acts like a **fertilizer**, making the soil richer and giving new plants a chance to grow. In fact, some seeds are adapted to fire and will only sprout after a fire has passed.

The thorns of a cactus are adaptations that help to prevent it from being eaten by grazing animals.

Roy Wittkuhn is a fire ecologist in Western Australia. He finds the work challenging and interesting. He says, "Just when you think you have a pattern or process figured out, you come across something that doesn't quite fit." There is always more to learn about the environment.

FIRESTARTER

The lodgepole pine tree of North America produces cones that are covered in resin, a hard waxy substance. If there is a fire in the forest the resin melts, releasing thousands of seeds. After the fire has passed, lodgepole pines are among the first trees to reappear.

Roy Wittkuhn checks out the growth of new plants in an area where there had been a fire 6 years before.

Find out about conserving Earth's resources on the next pages ...

THE IMPORTANCE OF CONSERVATION

Conservation is about protecting and managing Earth's natural resources. These resources include the world's living things, the places where they live, and the air and water that all life depends on. Metals, oil, coal, and other materials we take from the ground are also natural resources.

SUSTAINABLE DEVELOPMENT

One approach to conserving resources is called sustainable development. Sustainable development attempts to find ways of improving the quality of life for everyone today, while making sure that there are enough resources for the people of the future.

Somalian refugees queue for water at a standpipe. Water is a precious resource in many parts of the world.

These are some of the things we need to do to achieve sustainable development:

- Use **renewable energy** sources, such as wind power, rather than non-renewable ones, such as oil and other **fossil fuels**.
- Manage forests carefully and replant the trees we cut down.
- Do not take so many fish from the oceans that the fish numbers have no chance to recover.
- Avoid releasing chemicals into the environment that might prove harmful, such as **pesticides**.

THINK GLOBALLY, ACT LOCALLY

The French-American microbiologist and environmentalist René Dubos was very interested in the relationships between humans and their environment. He saw that the way to deal with big environmental problems was to start on a small scale. At a United Nations conference in 1972 he said that people should "think globally, act locally". Many people making small changes in their local surroundings, by recycling, for instance, could make a big difference to the world.

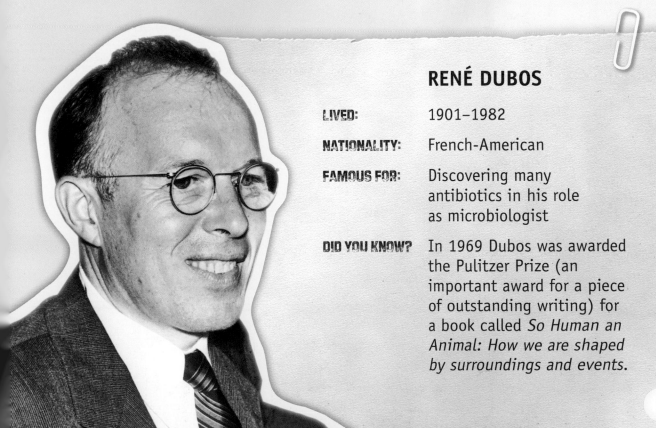

RENÉ DUBOS

LIVED:	1901–1982
NATIONALITY:	French-American
FAMOUS FOR:	Discovering many antibiotics in his role as microbiologist
DID YOU KNOW?	In 1969 Dubos was awarded the Pulitzer Prize (an important award for a piece of outstanding writing) for a book called *So Human an Animal: How we are shaped by surroundings and events*.

John Muir
conservation pioneer

John Muir was one of America's first **conservationists.** He believed that conservation wasn't just about using resources carefully. Natural beauty should be preserved for everyone to enjoy and wilderness areas should be left untouched as much as possible. His popular books describing America's wild places helped shape the way people thought about the environment.

EARLY DAYS

John Muir was born on 21 April 1838 in the small town of Dunbar, in Scotland. In 1849 the Muir family emigrated to the United States, eventually moving to Hickory Hill Farm near Portage, Wisconsin. Muir's father believed in hard work and John and his brother were kept busy on the farm from sunrise to sunset.

Theodore Roosevelt   John Muir

JOHN MUIR

LIVED: 1838–1914

NATIONALITY: Scottish-American

FAMOUS FOR: Encouraging the conservation of wild places and the setting up of national parks

DID YOU KNOW? As a young man Muir invented a device that tipped him out of bed before dawn, ready to get to work on the farm.

John Muir fell in love with California's Sierra Nevada and Yosemite. He wrote:

"It seemed to me the Sierra should be called ... the Range of Light ... the most divinely beautiful of all the mountain chains I have ever seen."

TRAVELLING MAN

Muir enrolled at the University of Wisconsin-Madison in 1860. Although he did not graduate he still learned a great deal. In 1867 an accident at work left Muir blind for a month. When he regained his sight, he became determined to see as much as possible of America's wild places. He walked from the northern United States all the way to the southern coast. He kept a journal of his trip that was later published as *A Thousand Mile Walk to the Gulf*. From there he sailed to Cuba and Panama and then along the Pacific coast to San Francisco.

OUR NATIONAL PARKS

In 1901, Muir published *Our National Parks*, a book that brought him to the attention of President Theodore Roosevelt. Roosevelt visited Muir in Yosemite National Park in 1903. Influenced by Muir, Roosevelt became one of the first US presidents to see conservation as an issue of national importance.

Muir made his home in California, but he continued to travel the world. Somehow he also found time to get married, raise a family, and successfully manage the family fruit ranch.

YELLOWSTONE
the first national park

In 1872 the United States government established the world's first national park in nearly 9,000 square kilometres (3,500 square miles) of land in the Yellowstone region of Wyoming. (A small part of the park also lies in the states of Montana and Idaho.) Yellowstone is a place of great natural beauty. Hundreds of different kinds of birds, mammals, reptiles, and other animals live in its forests, mountains, and rivers.

Every year, over 200 scientists are given permission to carry out research in Yellowstone Park. Permits are only granted under very strict guidelines designed to make sure that no damage is done to the park. Yellowstone researchers study not only the plants and animals in the park, but also the air, climate, soil, water, and the volcano!

WOLVES AND ELKS

In 1926 the last wolf in Yellowstone was killed. As a result, the numbers of elk (a type of deer) began to rise. In 1995 it was decided to bring wolves back to Yellowstone. As expected, the numbers of elk began to drop. But the numbers were dropping faster than they should have been. This was a puzzle. Scott Creel, ecology professor at Montana State University, wanted to find out what was happening.

What he discovered was that the elks had changed their diet. Instead of eating grass in the open meadows, they were eating shrubs in the forests, where they were less likely to be spotted by the wolves. However, the shrub diet was not as nutritious as the grass diet. The elk were having fewer calves because they were not getting as much to eat as before. That was why the numbers were falling.

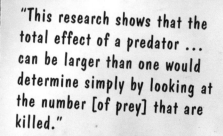

"This research shows that the total effect of a predator ... can be larger than one would determine simply by looking at the number [of prey] that are killed."

Scott Creel

SUPERVOLCANO

The many geysers, hot springs, and bubbling mudpools found in Yellowstone are a great attraction. Yellowstone lies over a supervolcano, the largest volcanic system in North America. The last major eruption took place over 600,000 years ago. Early in 2010 scientists were keeping a careful watch on a series of tiny earthquakes that shook Yellowstone Lake – just in case something bigger was about to take place.

Rachel Carson
Silent Spring

The US biologist and nature writer Rachel Carson was one of the first to draw attention to the danger of chemicals in the environment. She was born in the town of Springdale in the American state of Pennsylvania. From an early age she loved to write. When she left school she went to study English at the Pennsylvania College for Women, but later switched to her other great love, biology.

Carson started work with the US Bureau of Fisheries in 1935, writing scripts for a series of radio programmes about sea life. They were so impressed with her work that she was appointed to the full-time position of junior aquatic biologist, studying water-based organisms. She was only the second woman to be employed by the bureau at this level.

RACHEL CARSON

LIVED:	1907–1964
NATIONALITY:	American
FAMOUS FOR:	Starting the modern environmental movement
DID YOU KNOW?	Carson had her first story published in a magazine at the age of ten.

Rachel Carson loved to write and talk about her love of natural places.

In 1940 the bureau became the US Fish and Wildlife Service. Carson continued to write, developing a real talent for communicating science to ordinary people. One series of booklets, called Conservation in Action, looked at the wildlife and ecology of national wildlife refuges (places of safety). Eventually she became editor-in-chief of all Fish and Wildlife Service publications.

DDT

While working at the Fish and Wildlife Service, Carson had become concerned about the danger of pesticide use. One of the pesticides she was interested in was called DDT. She believed that this was having a harmful effect on fish and other wildlife. After spending years gathering information she decided to write about the problem in a book called *Silent Spring*.

The pesticide industry was furious and tried to discredit Carson's research. However, DDT was banned as a result of her findings. By bringing concerns about the environment to a wide readership, *Silent Spring* is credited with starting the modern environmental movement. The Rachel Carson National Wildlife Refuge on the coast of Maine was named in her honour in 1969.

THE CHEMICAL ENVIRONMENT

Rachel Carson's studies showed that chemicals can spread through the environment. Carried in the air and by water, they can move far from where they were actually released.

ENVIRONMENTAL CHEMISTRY

The science that looks at the ways in which chemicals behave in the environment is called environmental chemistry. Scientists use environmental chemistry to detect **pollutants** (harmful chemicals) and track them back to their source. Before they can do this, they have to understand how the environment works normally, before chemicals from human activities are released into it.

GREEN CHEMISTRY

Green chemistry is a branch of chemical engineering that tries to avoid producing pollution from chemical processes. Rather than finding ways of dealing with pollution, it tries to make sure that the pollution does not happen at all. One of the champions of green chemistry has been the Japanese scientist Ryoji Noyori.

Ryoji Noyori, one of the pioneers of green chemistry.

Dr Noyori has won many honours, including the Nobel Prize for Chemistry. In an interview he stated that his work was aimed at producing "useful substances and materials in an economical, energy saving and environmentally benign [harmless] way".

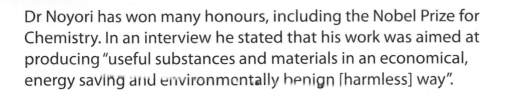

SAMPLER BEES

Jerry Bromenshenk, an environmental chemist at the University of Montana, enlisted some tiny helpers to gather samples of pollutants – honeybees. Bees cover a wide area as they forage for nectar. They come into contact with air, water, and soil, as well as plants. Bromenshenk says they are like "flying dust mops". When bees return to the hive, any pollutants they are carrying are released into the air inside the hive. By sampling the hive air, the scientists can discover what chemicals the bees have come in contact with.

Read about the dangers of using pesticides …

FOOD CHAINS AND WEBS

All living things need energy. Plants can capture the energy of sunlight. Animals get their energy from their food, by eating plants or other animals. The links along which energy moves from one living thing to another is called a food chain.

PRODUCERS AND CONSUMERS

Green plants are the first link in a food chain. Ecologists call green plants producers, because they use sunlight to produce the energy for everything else. Animals are called consumers, because they consume the energy that is captured by the plants.

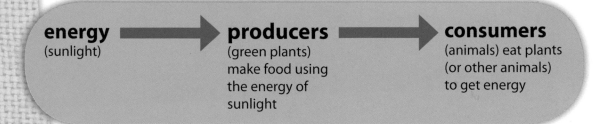

energy
(sunlight)

producers
(green plants)
make food using
the energy of
sunlight

consumers
(animals) eat plants
(or other animals)
to get energy

FOOD WEBS

Each plant and animal will usually appear in several different food chains. These food chains join together in a complex network called a food web. A food web is a way of showing all the different feeding relationships between living things in the environment.

"What we have to face is not an occasional dose of poison which has accidentally got into some article of food, but a persistent and continuous poisoning of the whole human environment."

Rachel Carson *Silent Spring*

PESTICIDES AND FOOD WEBS

One of the things that Rachel Carson wrote about in *Silent Spring* was the danger to larger animals, including humans, from the use of pesticides.

Imagine that a shrew catches and eats insects that have been poisoned by pesticides. Each insect only has a tiny dose of pesticide, but the shrew gets a much bigger dose by eating lots of insects. Further up the food chain, hawks catch and eat the shrews, and so get an even bigger dose of pesticide.

In *Silent Spring*, Carson spoke of hundreds of foxes dying in England because they had eaten poisoned birds and mice.

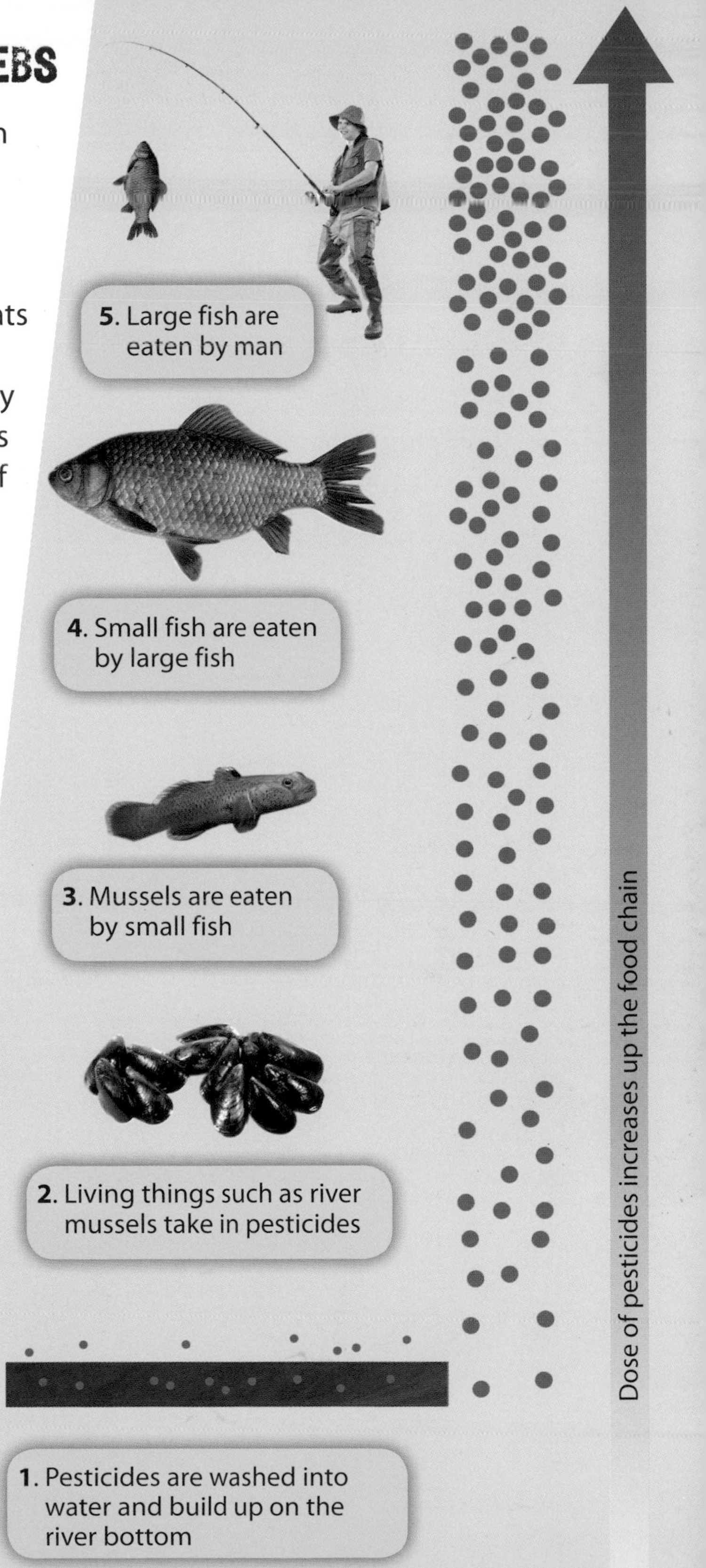

5. Large fish are eaten by man

4. Small fish are eaten by large fish

3. Mussels are eaten by small fish

2. Living things such as river mussels take in pesticides

1. Pesticides are washed into water and build up on the river bottom

This diagram shows the way that pesticides can build up in a food chain.

Dose of pesticides increases up the food chain

19

The view from SPACE

One of the most powerful boosts for the environmental movement came from far outside Earth itself. Humans first saw the whole Earth suspended in space when the *Apollo 8* astronauts looked back at it from the Moon in 1968. The photographs they took helped to raise awareness of Earth as an amazing living planet in the darkness of space.

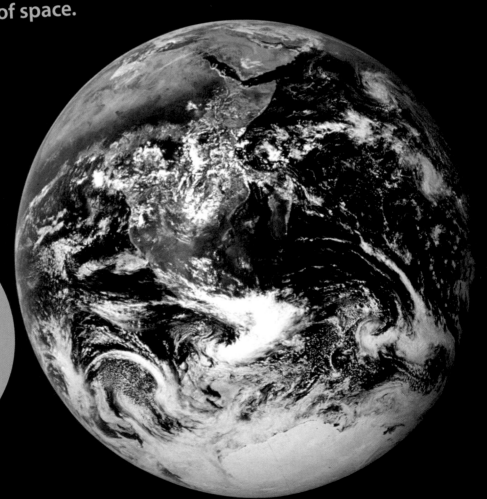

The Apollo 17 astronauts took this famous shot of the whole Earth in space on their way to the Moon in 1972.

THE EARTH OBSERVING SYSTEM

Today many satellites keep watch on Earth. The US **National Aeronautics and Space Administration (NASA)** runs an Earth Observing System (EOS). The EOS satellites monitor Earth's land and oceans, its atmosphere, and the living things that make their home there. Their mission is to develop a scientific understanding of Earth and how it responds to changes in the environment. These changes can be natural, such as erupting volcanoes, or caused by humans, such as the effects of our car exhausts and factories.

STUDENTS AND SPACE SCIENTISTS

The Dutch scientist Pieternel Levelt was one of the principal investigators for *Aura*, one of the EOS satellites. One of *Aura*'s tasks is to monitor air quality. In 2000 Levelt was approached by GLOBE, an international science programme that encourages thousands of students across the world to monitor the environment.

Many scientists were reluctant to use GLOBE observations, believing that high school students could not possibly take accurate measurements. Levelt believed that they could and set up an experiment to prove it. She compared measurements made by science professionals with those made by the students and found they were practically the same.

Being able to compare *Aura*'s observations from above with observations from the ground was enormously valuable. The GLOBE students were able to confirm the accuracy of the satellite readings.

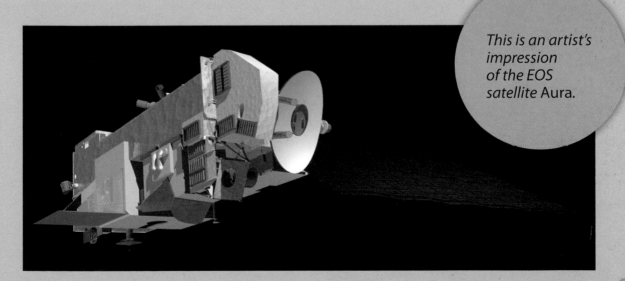

This is an artist's impression of the EOS satellite Aura.

James Lovelock
LIVING WORLDS

Independent scientist and researcher James Lovelock was born in Letchworth in Hertfordshire. He was a talented student who graduated with degrees in chemistry, medicine, and biophysics.

LIFE ON MARS

In the 1960s Lovelock worked together with scientists at NASA's Jet Propulsion Laboratory. The space agency was planning the *Viking* mission, a project to send probes to Mars. One of the things they wanted to look for on that planet was signs of life. Lovelock worked on developing sensitive instruments that would be used to examine the Martian atmosphere as well as the surface of the planet.

JAMES LOVELOCK

BORN:	1919
NATIONALITY:	British
FAMOUS FOR:	Proposing the Gaia **hypothesis** – the idea that Earth behaves as if it were a living planet
DID YOU KNOW?	Lovelock's laboratory is housed in a converted barn.

The Viking *landers found no traces of life in the harsh environment of Mars.*

Lovelock did not believe that the probes would find life on Mars. He came to this conclusion by studying the atmosphere of Mars. The oxygen present in Earth's atmosphere is largely due to the plant life here. Lovelock reasoned that if there was life on Mars then there should be oxygen in that planet's atmosphere, too. There was a lot of carbon dioxide in the Martian atmosphere, but there was very little oxygen. This was a sure sign to Lovelock that the planet was lifeless.

The *Viking* probes landed on Mars in 1976. They carried out tests on the Martian soil using experiments that Lovelock had helped to design. As Lovelock had predicted, no trace of life was found. Looking for life on Mars made him think about what other effects might be caused by the presence of life on a planet.

You can read more about Lovelock's work on the next pages ...

A LIVING PLANET?

Around 1972, James Lovelock first put forward the idea that the living and non-living parts of Earth could be thought of as a single, highly complex system. He suggested that life on Earth actually plays a part in shaping Earth's climate and atmosphere, maintaining the conditions that can support life.

GAIA

This complex system was given the name Gaia, after the Greek goddess of Earth. The idea that Earth could be thought of as a living planet was appealing to many in the environmental movement. Many scientists were sceptical, however, and the idea remains highly controversial.

The Earth goddess Gaia has been shown in different ways over the centuries. This version was painted by George Frederick Watts in 1895.

DAISYWORLD

Lovelock came up with a simple way to show how Gaia could work. Daisyworld is an imaginary planet where the only living things are black daisies and white daisies. How the daisies grow is affected by temperature. Black daisies absorb the Sun's heat, making conditions warmer, while white daisies reflect it, making things cooler.

If conditions are cool, black daisies thrive and raise the temperature. If conditions get too hot, the white daisies thrive and cool things down again. Acting together, the two daisies keep the temperature within a comfortable range.

Lovelock went on to make more complicated models, with different types of daisy and animals to eat the daisies, and each other. He still found that conditions on Daisyworld were kept within balance.

1. Similar numbers of different daisies

2. More black daisies live in cool conditions, black daisies raise the temperature

3. More white daisies grow

THE REVENGE OF GAIA

In 2006 Lovelock wrote a book called *The Revenge of Gaia*. In it he suggested that damage done to the environment by human activities was weakening Earth's ability to maintain ideal conditions for life. One possibility is that there will be runaway **global warming**, with temperatures increasing rapidly.

CAPTURING CFCS

In 1956 James Lovelock invented a sensitive device called an electron capture detector. This was used for detecting chemicals in the atmosphere. Using this device, Lovelock was one of the first to detect pollutants called CFCs. These are chemicals that were widely used in the manufacture of refrigerators, for example. He found CFCs in every single air sample he took, from the northern hemisphere down to the Antarctic. However, Lovelock did not believe the CFCs were a hazard.

CFCS AND OZONE

In 1974 scientists F. Sherwood Rowland and Mario Molina announced that CFCs were not so harmless after all. **Ozone** is a type of oxygen that forms a layer high in the atmosphere. It is very important to life on Earth because it blocks harmful ultraviolet rays from the Sun. Rowland and Molina had discovered that the CFCs broke up in the upper atmosphere, and as they did so they destroyed the ozone. The two scientists were later to receive the Nobel Prize for their work in identifying this potentially catastrophic problem.

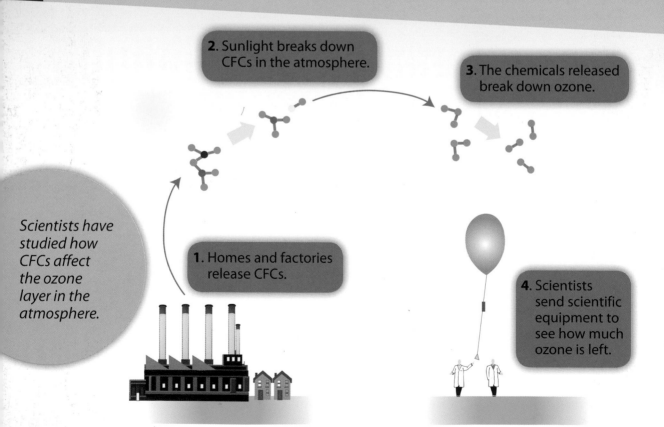

2. Sunlight breaks down CFCs in the atmosphere.

3. The chemicals released break down ozone.

Scientists have studied how CFCs affect the ozone layer in the atmosphere.

1. Homes and factories release CFCs.

4. Scientists send scientific equipment to see how much ozone is left.

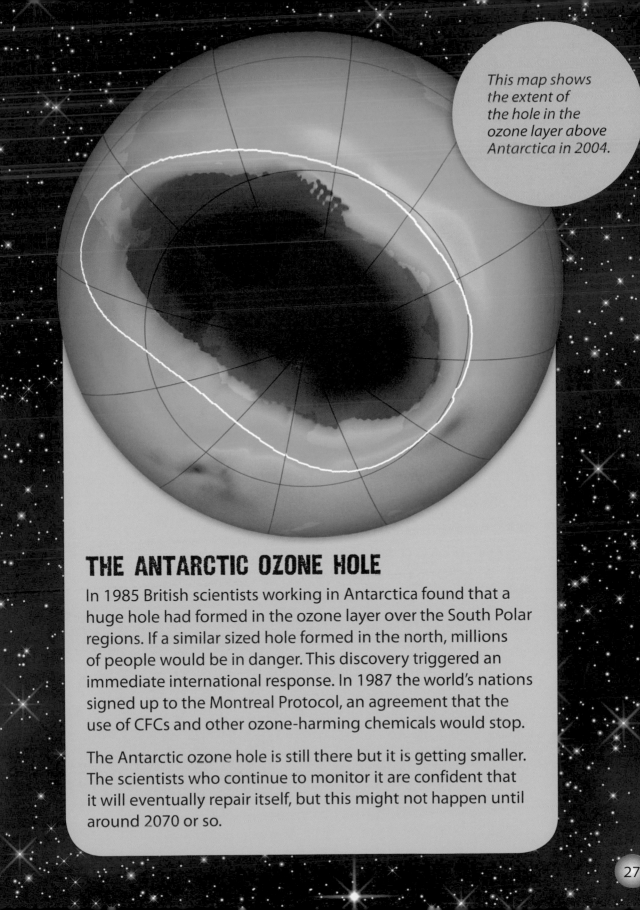

This map shows the extent of the hole in the ozone layer above Antarctica in 2004.

THE ANTARCTIC OZONE HOLE

In 1985 British scientists working in Antarctica found that a huge hole had formed in the ozone layer over the South Polar regions. If a similar sized hole formed in the north, millions of people would be in danger. This discovery triggered an immediate international response. In 1987 the world's nations signed up to the Montreal Protocol, an agreement that the use of CFCs and other ozone-harming chemicals would stop.

The Antarctic ozone hole is still there but it is getting smaller. The scientists who continue to monitor it are confident that it will eventually repair itself, but this might not happen until around 2070 or so.

James Hansen
CLIMATE WATCHER

Like James Lovelock, NASA scientist James Hansen gained insights into Earth's environment by studying another world. In this case the place in question was the planet Venus.

SISTER PLANET

Hansen was involved in studying the planet Venus in the 1960s and 70s. Venus is sometimes called Earth's sister planet because the two planets are very similar in size. However, conditions there are very different. Sulphuric acid droplets in a dense atmosphere of carbon dioxide blanket a barren desert landscape that bakes at a temperature of 480 °C (900 °F).

Why is Venus so hot? It is hotter even than Mercury, the planet closest to the Sun. Hansen thought it was because of its atmosphere. He suggested that the gases in the atmosphere of Venus trapped heat. This resulted in a **greenhouse effect** that caused the high temperatures on the surface of the planet.

Planet	Distance from the Sun	Temperature
Mercury	58 million km (36 million miles)	450 °C (800 °F) daytime
Venus	108 million km (67 million miles)	480 °C (900 °F)
Earth	149 million km (93 million miles)	15 °C (52 °F)

JAMES HANSEN

BORN:	1941
NATIONALITY:	American
FAMOUS FOR:	Warning that the Earth's temperature is increasing
DID YOU KNOW?	Hansen called for fuel company bosses to be put on trial for "crimes against humanity and nature".

THE GREENHOUSE EFFECT

Energy from the Sun warms the surface of Earth. Some of this heat is reflected back into space.

Earth's atmosphere naturally contains gases such as water vapour, methane, and carbon dioxide. These gases trap some of the reflected heat and keep Earth warmer than it would be otherwise. **They are called greenhouse gases, and the warming they cause is called the greenhouse effect.**

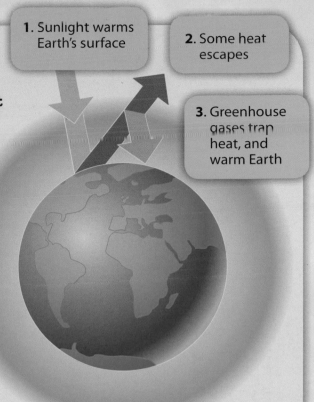

1. Sunlight warms Earth's surface

2. Some heat escapes

3. Greenhouse gases trap heat, and warm Earth

EARLY WARNING

The Swedish scientist Svante Arrhenius was the first to see that the greenhouse effect could cause problems for us. As early as 1906 he predicted that the carbon dioxide produced by burning fossil fuels would cause global warming.

TAKING THE WORLD'S TEMPERATURE

In 1987 Hansen published details of a survey of temperatures taken from weather stations around the world. He and his fellow researchers looked at records dating from 1880 to 1985. They found that the average global temperature had gone up between 0.5 and 0.7 °C (0.9 and 1.26 °F) over the 100-year period and that the four warmest years recorded (up until then) were all in the 1980s. Later observations confirmed the continuing rise in temperature. Hansen was convinced that it was caused by human activity.

CLIMATE CHANGE

Most environmental scientists are convinced that global warming and the **climate change** that results from it are among the most important issues facing us today. A great deal of research is going into discovering how quickly Earth's temperature is rising, whether it is being caused by natural events or by the activities of humans, and what might be done to stop it.

NASA's Glory satellite will collect data on aerosols that could play a part in climate change.

WHAT IS CLIMATE CHANGE?

Climate is the long-term average weather conditions in an area. The types of plants and animals that can live in an area depend on the climate there. Many scientists are convinced that the warming of Earth will cause shifting wind patterns and changes in rainfall, for example, and that this will have an effect on climate.

CARS AND CLIMATE

Dr Nadine Unger of NASA's Goddard Institute for Space Studies has been looking at the effect different human activities have on climate. It is a complex picture. <u>Some chemicals can cause warming of the atmosphere, but others can have a cooling effect</u>.

For example, Dr Unger points out that industries burn fuel that releases carbon dioxide, which causes greenhouse warming. But they also release sulphates, which are chemicals that enter the atmosphere in the form of tiny particles called **aerosols**. These can cause cooling by blocking heat from the Sun and by changing clouds to make them brighter so they reflect heat back into space. The cooling effect from the aerosols actually outweighs the warming effect from the carbon dioxide.

Cars, trucks, and other vehicles also burn fuel and emit carbon dioxide and other greenhouse chemicals. However, they emit very little sulphates. According to Dr Unger, transport is having a much bigger effect on climate change than industry.

"There's a large amount of uncertainty about how aerosols affect climate, especially through the indirect effects on clouds. Hopefully, NASA's Glory mission will help reduce the uncertainties associated with aerosols."

Nadine Unger

Nadine Unger studies the way human activities affect climate.

A NUCLEAR SOLUTION?

For some people, nuclear power is one of the most dangerous ways of producing energy. For others, it is a clean and safe source of energy.

"I am in favour of nuclear energy for small, densely populated nations such as the UK ... Such nations need an abundant supply of electricity to continue civilized life, and there is no alternative to nuclear energy ... [It] also happens to be the safest, the most economical and reliable of energy sources. It is foolish to reject it."

James Lovelock (see page 22)

M HP 66.53MW

Nuclear power stations are controlled by complex technology.

THE CASE FOR NUCLEAR POWER

Those who are for nuclear power point to its greater energy production. A nuclear power station will use around 50 tonnes of uranium a year, but a coal-fired station will use over 500 tonnes of coal every hour.

For scientists like James Hansen (see page 28), one of the most important reasons for switching our energy production away from fossil fuels to nuclear power is that nuclear power does not produce carbon dioxide. It could be an essential move in the battle against global warming.

THE CASE AGAINST NUCLEAR POWER

Others disagree, of course. Green activists have always campaigned against the use of nuclear power. Those who are against it are concerned about the dangers of **radiation** (nuclear energy, which travels in the form of waves or particles) and the problems with safely disposing of radioactive waste.

There is also the argument that nuclear power could only provide a small part of the energy we use. For example, it could not be used to power cars, trains, or aircraft. People also argue that nuclear power is slow and expensive. It would not be used enough to help reduce climate change.

Many environmentalists would prefer it if more money were spent on renewable energy sources such as wind farms and tide power. The best solution is likely to involve using a number of different energy sources, including nuclear power.

The engineers standing next to the blades of a wind turbine show how big it is.

VANDANA SHIVA CONSERVATION FARMING

The Indian environmentalist Vandana Shiva has been active for many years, exploring the environmental effects of the "green revolution" in agriculture and the use of genetically modified crops.

VANDANA SHIVA

BORN: 1952

NATIONALITY: Indian

FAMOUS FOR: Showing the importance of diversity, including biodiversity, diversity among people, and diversity of knowledge

DID YOU KNOW? In 2003 *Time* magazine described Vandana Shiva as an environmental hero.

"To me, fighting for people's rights, protecting nature, protecting diversity is a constant reminder of that which is so valuable in life."

Vandana Shiva

This scientist is developing crops for the green revolution.

Vandana Shiva was born in Dehra Dun, India. Her father was a forester and her mother was a farmer, so it is no surprise that she had an early love of nature. Her early training was as a physicist, however. She obtained a doctorate in particle physics at the University of Western Ontario, Canada, in 1978.

On a trip back to India, her interest in the environment began to grow when she discovered that a forest she had loved as a child had been cleared. In 1982, having returned to live in India, she set up a research foundation to help ordinary people come to terms with environmental problems. To begin with, the foundation operated from her mother's cowshed.

Shiva campaigned against the green revolution (see panel). She argued that **native** plants, which were better adapted to local conditions, were being lost. The increased use of chemicals was causing pollution. Farmers who could not afford the expensive fertilizers were actually getting poorer crops than before.

THE GREEN REVOLUTION

The green revolution began in the 1940s. It involved the introduction of new types of food grain, such as wheat, into developing countries such as India and Mexico. These new varieties produced bigger crops, but they needed large amounts of fertilizers and pesticides.

The part of South East Asia where this orang-utan lives is a region of great biodiversity.

BIODIVERSITY

Biodiversity means the variety of living things found in a particular place. Some places have greater biodiversity than others. There are many more different forms of life in a rainforest than there are in a desert, for example. The goal of conservationists is to preserve biodiversity as far as possible.

NEW GIFT

Biodiversity has been one of Vandana Shiva's long-term interests. In 1991 she founded Navdanya, which means "Nine Seeds" or "New Gift". The aim of this project was to provide an alternative to the "green revolution" crops. Over 40 seed banks were set up to preserve local varieties. Farmers were encouraged to plant crops that grew well without the need for chemical fertilizers and pesticides. Shiva also argued that the greater variety there was, the more chance there was of having crops that could survive climate change.

BIOPIRACY

In 1997 Vandana Shiva wrote a book called *Biopiracy.* For many years, scientists have travelled the world looking for plants and animals that could be used for our benefit, as food or medicine, for example. In her book, Shiva accused big companies from richer, more developed countries of taking samples of plants and animals for research from poorer countries. She said they did this without asking permission and without sharing any of the rewards. This was what she referred to as biopiracy.

Martha, the last passenger pigeon. A bird that once numbered in the billions became extinct when Martha died in 1914.

Wangari Maathai
GRASSROOTS CAMPAIGNER

The environmental campaigner Wangari Maathai was the first East African woman to be awarded the Nobel Peace Prize. In the 1970s she founded the Green Belt Movement, dedicated to tree planting, women's rights, and environmental conservation.

Wangari Maathai plants trees with some of the women of the Green Belt Movement.

WANGARI MAATHAI

LIVED: 1940–2011

NATIONALITY: Kenyan

FAMOUS FOR: Organizing women in Africa to help protect the environment

DID YOU KNOW? Barack Obama planted a tree with Maathai when he visited Kenya in 2006.

Wangari Maathai was born in the village of Ihithe in Kenya. After completing high school she went to study in the United States, where she obtained a degree in biological sciences. She returned to Kenya and in 1971 the University of Nairobi awarded her a doctorate. She was the first East African woman to achieve this.

THE GREEN BELT MOVEMENT

Maathai joined the National Council of Women of Kenya. It was here that she formed the idea that women could help to improve the environment by planting trees. By 1977 the idea had grown into the Green Belt Movement. Maathai encouraged women to plant trees using seeds from nearby forests so the trees would be native to the area.

Planting trees brings many benefits. It provides a source of food and fuel; it prevents **deforestation**; it helps people to learn skills and earn an income. Since it was founded, the Green Belt Movement has trained over 30,000 women in forestry and other skills. Over 40 million trees have been planted by Kenyan women. Other African countries have been encouraged by the Green Belt Movement's success and have set up similar schemes of their own.

PEOPLE AND PLANET

Environmentalists such as Wangari Maathai and Vandana Shiva have shown how ordinary people can become involved in protecting the environment. Maathai, in particular, wants to see young people involved in environmental activities. She encourages them to look for new ways of protecting habitats and managing resources.

"I would like to call on young people to commit themselves to activities that contribute toward achieving their long-term dreams. They have the energy and creativity to shape a sustainable future. To the young people I say, you are a gift to your communities and indeed the world. You are our hope and our future."

Wangari Maathai, in her Nobel Prize acceptance speech, 2004

ANSWERS AND QUESTIONS

Scientists all over the world continue to find out new things about the environment. Through their discoveries they can try to tell us how it works and they can warn us about things that might go wrong. Perhaps they might also give us some ideas about how to put things right.

OUR WORLD

One important thing that environmental scientists have shown us is the way that things are linked together. Aerosols from factories can be carried around the world, pesticides can spread far from where they were used.

We might not all be scientists but we can all be aware of what's going on in our environment. And we should be aware that we can have an effect on that environment. Remember to "think globally, act locally". If we are to have a sustainable future and a decent environment, everyone has to be committed and work together.

These students are testing the quality of the water in a river.

TIMELINE

1872
Yellowstone, the first national park, is created by US president Ulysses S. Grant

1892
The Sierra Club is founded, with John Muir as its first president

1914
Martha, the last living passenger pigeon, dies – a species that once numbered in the billions is now extinct

1968
The *Apollo 8* astronauts send back the first pictures of Earth seen from the Moon

1962
Rachel Carson's *Silent Spring* calls attention to the danger of chemicals being released into the environment

1961
The World Wildlife Fund (later the Worldwide Fund for Nature) is founded

1969
The environmental organization Friends of the Earth is founded

1970
Millions of people gather for the first Earth Day to protest about damage being done to the environment and bring their concerns to the attention of politicians

1972
René Dubos and Barbara Ward publish *Only One Earth*, a book that warns that human activity is putting at risk Earth's ability to support us

1985

Scientists from the British Antarctic Survey report the discovery of a hole in the ozone layer above Antarctica

1983

The United States Environmental Protection Agency reports that the build-up of greenhouse gases in the atmosphere is likely to lead to global warming

1974

F. Sherwood Rowland and Mario Molina publish their discovery that CFCs are destroying the ozone layer

1972

James Lovelock puts forward his Gaia hypothesis

1987

The Montreal Protocol aims at stopping the production of chemicals that destroy ozone

1991

Vandana Shiva founds Navdanya in India, a project to provide an alternative to "green revolution" crops and chemicals

1992

At the Earth Summit in Rio de Janeiro, Brazil, most countries agree to adopt Agenda 21, which calls for sustainable development by using natural resources more efficiently, reducing pollutants and chemical waste, and taking other measures to protect the environment

2009

World governments meet in Copenhagen to decide on a plan for dealing with climate change but fail to reach agreement.

2004

Wangari Maathai is awarded the Nobel Prize for her work with the Green Belt Movement in Kenya

1995

The Intergovernmental Panel on Climate Change reports that "the balance of evidence suggests that there is a discernible human influence on global climate"

Glossary

adaptation something that makes a living thing suited to its environment. The thick fur of a polar bear is an adaptation to the cold conditions of the Arctic.

aerosol tiny solid or liquid particle that is suspended in a gas. Smoke is a type of aerosol.

biodiversity the variety of different living things that are found in an area

climate change changes in Earth's climate, particularly those thought to result from global warming

conservationist someone who believes in protecting natural places and the living things found there

deforestation process of destroying a forest

ecology relationships between living things and their environment

fertilizer a substance that is added to soil to help plants to grow better

fossil fuel fuel formed in the ground over millions of years from the remains of dead plants and animals. Coal, petroleum, and natural gas are all fossil fuels.

geology the scientific study of the origin, history, composition, and structure of Earth

global warming the increase in the average temperature of Earth, thought to be caused by the greenhouse effect

greenhouse effect warming that takes place in the atmosphere when heat is trapped by greenhouse gases

greenhouse gas a gas in the atmosphere that absorbs heat and sends it back to Earth rather than letting it escape into space

hypothesis idea, or explanation as to why certain things have happened

NASA National Aeronautics and Space Administration, the US organization that conducts space exploration, scientific discovery, and aeronautics research

native describes plants or animals found naturally in an area; those brought in by humans are said to have been introduced

ozone a type of oxygen found high in the atmosphere that filters out much of the harmful ultraviolet radiation from the Sun

pesticide chemical that is used to kill pests

pollutant unwanted, often harmful, chemical found in the environment as a result of human activities

radiation energy that travels in the form of waves or particles. High-energy radiation can be very damaging to living things.

renewable energy energy obtained from sources that are naturally replaced, such as the energy from the wind or the Sun

Match the scientist to the place

1 James Hansen

2 Pieternel Levelt

3 James Lovelock

4 Wangari Maathai

5 John Muir

6 F. Sherwood Rowland and Mario Molina

7 Vandana Shiva

8 Roy Wittkuhn

(a) Daisyworld

(b) India

(c) Kenya

(d) ozone layer

(e) space

(f) Venus

(g) Western Australia

(h) Yosemite

Answers: 1 (f), **2** (e), **3** (a), **4** (c), **5** (h), **6** (d), **7** (b), **8** (g)

Find out more

Books

Climate Change, John Woodward (Dorling Kindersley, 2008)

Earth in the Hot Seat: Bulletins from a Warming World, Marfe Ferguson Delano (National Geographic Society, 2009)

Gaia Warriors, Nicola Davies (Walker, 2009)

John Muir: Preserving and Protecting the Environment, Henry Eliot (Crabtree, 2009)

Mama Miti: Wangari Maathai and the Trees of Kenya, Donna Jo Napoli (Simon and Schuster, 2010)

Nuclear Power (Energy Now and in the Future), Neil Morris (Franklin Watts, 2009)

Ozone Hole (Earth SOS), Sally Morgan (Franklin Watts, 2007)

Protecting the Planet: Environmental Activism (Green Generation), Pamela Dell (Compass Point, 2010)

Recycling (Do It Yourself), Anna Claybourne (Heinemann Library, 2008)

Tree of Life: The Incredible Biodiversity of Life on Earth, Rochelle Strauss (A&C Black, 2005)

Yellowstone National Park, Bobbie Kalman (Crabtree, 2009)

DVDs

The 11th Hour, a documentary produced and narrated by Leonardo DiCaprio, on the state of the natural environment. Warner Home Video, 2008

The Age of Stupid, a film starring Pete Postlethwaite asking the question: "Why didn't we stop climate change when we still had the chance?" Dogwoof Ltd, 2009

The Truth about Climate Change, David Attenborough, Eureka Entertainment, 2008

The Vanishing of the Bees, a documentary that examines the declining bee population and what this means for the relationship between people and the environment. Dogwoof Ltd, 2010

Websites

The website of the Natural Environment Research Council, dedicated to increasing our knowledge and understanding of the natural world
www.nerc.ac.uk

Kids Do Ecology – a colourful introduction to the science of ecology, including careers in ecology and what being an ecologist is really like
kids.nceas.ucsb.edu

A comprehensive guide to the topics associated with sustainable development
www.ace.mmu.ac.uk/esd

The life and work of John Muir
www.sierraclub.org/john_muir_exhibit

A website dedicated to the life and legacy of Rachel Carson
www.rachelcarson.org

The website of the Greenbelt Movement and its founder, Wangari Maathai
www.greenbeltmovement.org

Places to visit

Eden Project
Bodelva
St Austell
Cornwall PL24 2SG
Learn a lot about plants and their importance to people and the environment at this huge visitor centre.

Centre for Alternative Technology
Llwyngwern
Machynlleth
Powys SY20 9AZ
This centre offers solutions to challenges such as climate change, pollution, and the waste of precious resources, with interactive displays and organic gardens.

Index